GLOW GIRL!

Empowering Teenage Girls to Grow, Lead, Overcome, and Win!

MIA HALL

Glow Girl! Empowering Teenage Girls to Grow, Lead, Overcome, and Win!

For permission requests or more information, please email: mianhall@gmail.com.

Library of Congress Control Number: 2025915787
Paperback ISBN: 979-8-9994838-0-5
Hardback ISBN: 979-8-9994838-8-1
E-book ISBN: 979-8-9994838-1-2
Cover Photo Shot by: Alongside Multimedia Agency

Printed in the United States of America

Disclaimer

The information in this book is for educational and informational purposes only. The author and publisher are not licensed counselors, therapists, or medical professionals. This book is not intended to provide, nor should it be construed as, professional mental health, legal, or medical advice.

Readers are encouraged to consult qualified professionals before making any decisions regarding personal development, mental health, or medical treatment. Any reliance on the information in this book is at the reader's own discretion and risk.

The author and publisher have made every effort to ensure the accuracy of the information at the time of printing. They do not assume, and hereby disclaim, any liability for any loss, damage, or disruption caused by errors or omissions, whether due to negligence, accident, or any other cause.

The responsibility for complying with all applicable laws and regulations—whether international, federal, state, or local, covering professional licensing, business practices, advertising, and any other aspect of doing business in the United States, Canada, or other jurisdictions—rests solely with the reader and consumer.

Any references to people, events, or experiences are either used with permission, are fictionalized for illustrative purposes, or are the author's personal reflections.

Any perceived offense or slight to individuals or organizations is entirely unintentional.

Dedication

I dedicate this book to the first Brown Girl I ever saw "GLOW" in action—my mom.

The sacrifices she made over the years have inspired me to live to my fullest potential

and to motivate others to do the same.

Foreword

By Dr. Gabby Cudjoe Wilkes

Ready to GLOW? And I mean *really* glow? Then this book is for you.

I've always been captivated by the idea of things that glow in the dark—the objects that sit quietly when the lights are on but come alive when darkness hits. They don't change who they are; they just become more visible. They stand out in the most amazing way. It's like the glow was always there. You just couldn't see it until the moment was right.

That's what this book is all about: showing you how to be that light, wherever you are—how to *GLOW* no matter what life throws your way.

Did you know glow-in-the-dark objects are photoluminescent? They literally absorb light to produce their own glow. Some shine for a moment; others keep glowing—as long as they're fed with energy. This book is your source of that energizing light. Once you start, you'll never stop shining.

But here's the thing: it's not enough to *want* to glow. You have to plan for it. You have to decide that glowing is your goal. Like Mia Hall says, "Setting goals is like choosing your destination—it gives you direction."

I've known Mia for over twenty years, ever since we met at Hampton University. She's always been about those big dreams and bigger goals—whether it was graduate school, basketball, entertainment journalism, or taking her place in front of the camera—from Harvard to the New York Knicks, Black Enterprise to NBC, red carpets to the director's seat, Mia has always had a clear path forward. In *Glow Girl*, she's showing *us* how to walk it, too.

What makes *Glow Girl* even more special is Mia's honesty. She's not just talking about success—she's sharing her process. Her journey. Her lessons. From growing up in Brooklyn to leaning on mentors and community programs, Mia's story is a masterclass in resilience. And she wants you to know that if she can do it, so can you.

I've had the privilege of knowing Mia in both her biggest moments and her most vulnerable ones. As a pastor for over a decade, I've seen what true character looks like. Mia's integrity has never wavered. Whether she's celebrating a win or weathering a storm, she glows.

In *Glow Girl*, she invites you into the mindset behind her success: grit, grace, and a whole lot of heart.

Every young woman needs this book. Honestly, I'd recommend it for women of any age. If you're ready to build resilience, walk boldly in your calling, and stay grounded in your worth—this is your guide.

Glow, girl. GLOW.

Contents

Introduction

Origin

Growing up, I loved fireflies.

Have you ever seen one up close? That little flicker of light in the dark feels magical—like God dropped tiny stars in the grass just for us to chase. Back in the day, my cousin, friends, and I would run through Pink Houses Projects in East New York, laughing, playing double dutch, getting 'Tropical Fantasy' drinks and Wise potato chips from the corner store. But when those streetlights blinked on? You already know—we were supposed to go inside.

But not when the fireflies came out.

That was different. That meant summer had officially begun. It meant maybe—just maybe—we could beg for a few more minutes outside, a few more chances to catch those glowing beauties before bedtime.

And you know what? I'm grateful my mom and grandmother— my whole family, really—let me stay out a little longer sometimes. Not because they didn't care about rules but because they did care about *wonder*. They knew that chasing those fireflies wasn't just about bugs. It was about chasing curiosity... chasing the idea that something ordinary, like a little girl from the Projects, could glow in the dark too.

And, friend... that same light? Guess what? It's in you, too.

As an entertainment producer, I see firsthand how the media often promotes narrow, unrealistic standards of beauty. Too often, young women are bombarded with images that misrepresent them— or leave them out entirely. When you rarely see girls with your skin tone, hair texture, or body type being celebrated, it can send the false message that you're not enough.

But let me be clear: that's a lie. You are beautiful exactly as you are. Your beauty is defined by your authenticity, your culture, your joy, and your light—not filtered images or Eurocentric ideals.

If you picked up this book, you're ready to GLOW: Grow, Lead, Overcome, and Win—and yes, you absolutely can. Everything you need to shine is already within you. You can achieve some of your biggest dreams and inspire others along the way. This book is here to help you unlock that light.

I wrote this book because I've been where you are. I know what it feels like to suffer from self-doubt, fear of failure (and even success), and wondering if you're enough. But here's the truth: you are more than enough.

Discovering your unique gifts and building the foundation for the life you desire—and the impact you're meant to make—isn't easy, but it's possible.

When I used to watch shows and movies where characters went to Harvard University on my grandmother's tiny TV, stacked on top of another larger, broken TV, I never imagined I could go there. But at 21, I earned my master's degree from Harvard's Graduate School of Education.

Why This Book Exists

I founded Brown Girls Glow in 2018 after my speaking coaches, Eric Thomas, PhD, and CJ Quinney, encouraged me to invest in teenage girls, just as programs like PowerPlay NYC poured into me. At first, I wasn't sure. I had been working with college grads at the time in my early thirties to help them land dream jobs, and I didn't know if I wanted to shift gears. But as I reflected on why I went into education in the first place—my curiosity about what helps some students thrive while others from similar backgrounds struggle—the vision became clear.

I wanted to create something that would guide young women through life's challenges, equip them with tools to overcome, and help them rise with purpose.

This book is that guide. It's for navigating life as a young woman. It's filled with the lessons high school didn't teach me. I'll show you how I shifted my mindset, overcame setbacks, and kept pushing forward—even when things got tough.

Glow Girl isn't just about dreaming big (though it will do that). It's about giving you the tools to turn your dreams into reality. You'll learn how to embrace your uniqueness, build community, focus on your strengths, and rise above whatever comes your way.

Why You Matter

Before we begin, I want you to know something important: you matter. You were created with unique gifts and talents the world needs—gifts only you can offer. Your life has a purpose, and this book is here to help you discover it.

Glow Girl is about becoming your best self, not a perfect version of you. It's about growing through life's challenges and letting your light shine from the inside out.

Let's get started. Read this book with an open heart and mind. Take the lessons that resonate with you and reflect on the questions at the end of each chapter. And most of all, believe in yourself.

This is your time to GLOW.

Glow Girl

Glow Girl. Shine from the inside out.
Carry confidence, not comparison.
Lead with kindness, not competition.
Know your worth, even on the days you don't feel it.
Know that your glow isn't just beauty—it's bravery, purpose, and
resilience.

This book will help you discover your own glow—
the kind that can't be dimmed, no matter what life throws your
way.

PART 1
GROW

1. Know Yourself to Grow Yourself

Education was always my 'thing.'

Growing up, my family didn't have a lot of money, but my mom would always buy me an educational toy every Christmas—like a Speak and Spell (an electronic spelling machine), a kid calculator, or a stack of books. My family, which included four adults and two children, lived in a two-bedroom apartment in a housing development (also known as the Projects), and it was *filled* with books. Shelves lined nearly every wall in every room, overflowing with stories and learning tools.

My grandmother, who was retired, read the newspaper every single day. Education was always a cornerstone in our household. Even though our neighborhood lacked resources, my family signed me up for anything they thought might enrich me or my younger cousin's life. I took dance classes at the East New York Theatrical Workshop, joined Girl Scouts (led by my Aunt Elvera), attended a faith-based after-school show called Yogi Bear (now Metro World Kids), and participated in creative programs at the Pink Houses Community Center.

In my early 20s, one of my mentors, Gloria—a former history teacher—recommended I read *Why You Act the Way You Do* by Tim LaHaye. That book opened a new world for me. I learned that my drive to study hard and perform well in school wasn't just about upbringing or environment—it was part of my temperament.

According to Britannica, *temperament* refers to personality traits that affect how we emotionally respond to life. Tim LaHaye's model, based on Galen's ancient theories, outlines four classic temperaments.

Learning that certain parts of my personality were recognized as human behavior, and not solely based on my choices, upbringing, or environment, really opened my mind. They helped me understand myself and answered questions about my identity. I no longer beat myself up for things I couldn't change—I started managing my weaknesses and leaning into my strengths. There really can be a reason why you do what you do, and it might be built into your temperament.

Below are the basic types—see which ones resonate most with you:

STRENGTHS AND WEAKNESSES OF EACH TEMPERAMENT TYPE

SANGUINE

Enthusiastic, sociable optimistic, playful creative

Disorganized, lacks focus

CHOLERIC

Ambitious, confident, decisive, strong-willed leader

Impulsive, aggressive, impatient, insensitive

PHLEGMATIC

Calm, patient, diplomatic, reliable

Indecisive, unassertive, passive, apathetic

MELANCHOLIC

Analytical, detail-oriented loyal, empathetic, thoughtful

Pessimistic, moody self-critical, anxious

It is perfectly fine if two temperaments resonate! Most of us have a dominant trait and a secondary one. For example, I most identify with the Sanguine temperament with a touch of Phlegmatic.

Understanding your temperament can be empowering. It can boost your self-esteem and reduce the urge to compare yourself to others who we believe are doing better than us. Often, we struggle with low confidence because we think we are "behind" someone else—but maybe we are just different. And different does not mean less than.

The truth is, you are phenomenal just as you are. You might be different from other students in your school, your family, or your coworkers, but that difference isn't always a result of your choices. It can stem from your personality type, which can be shaped more by how you were created than anything else.

Other popular personality frameworks include:

- Myers-Briggs Type Indicator (MBTI)
- DISC: Dominance, Influence, Steadiness, Conscientiousness
- Type A, B, C, and D personalities

Let's take one concept many people relate to: Introversion vs. Extroversion (via *Britannica*):

- Introvert: Reserved, introspective, enjoys solitude
- Extrovert: Outgoing, energetic, seeks social interaction
- Ambivert: A blend of both traits

I am an ambivert. Learning that helped me avoid "FOMO"—the Fear of Missing Out. I realized staying home didn't mean I was missing out; sometimes it meant I was honoring my energy and something was not for me.

Fawn Weaver, founder of Uncle Nearest Whiskey, once told me about reading *Please Understand Me II*. When she discovered that only 1% of people thought like her, she stopped needing others to understand her. That stuck with me.

Glitter Dust

You were created uniquely, exactly the way you are, for a specific reason. There is a problem on Earth that only your skills, perspective, and personality can solve.

Comparison is the thief of joy. Stay in your lane. I once drove through gridlock traffic in Atlanta and kept switching lanes to get ahead. But every time I switched, the lane slowed down. Life is like that. Sometimes staying in your own lane is the fastest route forward.

Understanding my personality helped me embrace who I am. That self-awareness gave me confidence, and that confidence allowed me to dream big and believe I could accomplish anything I set my mind to.

Your story matters, too. You do not have to follow anyone else's script. Let's reflect on how your path is unfolding—and how staying in your lane might actually get you there faster.

You matter. You are important.

Reflections

1. What are your unique gifts?

2. What are the personality traits that you need to look out for?

3. Do you notice personality temperaments that may relate to your friends?

4. How will learning more about your personality boost your self-esteem?

2. Tend to Your Soil

Mindset Matters

Mindset Determines Your Attitude.

Attitude Determines Approach.

Approach Determines Success or Failure.

I remember sitting in service at Christian Cultural Center (Christian Life Center at that time) when I first heard the importance of mindset emphasized. Dr. A.R. Bernard, Sr., frequently shared how we can renew our minds by taking in new information.

This came from one of my favorite scriptures: *"Do not be conformed to this world, but be transformed by the renewal of your mind, that by testing you may discern what is the will of God, what is good and acceptable and perfect." – Romans 12:2.*

From Chapter 1, you know that I've always enjoyed studying. So, learning that we can "renew our minds" through studying was exciting for me. It became something I made sure to do whenever I needed to grow in a particular area of my life. At the time I learned this, I had just completed my first year at Russell Sage Middle School. It was a significant transition and one I did not handle well.

I didn't follow the right crowd. Throughout grade school, I had been in gifted classes, but by the end of my first year in middle school, my grades were so poor that I failed out of the honors program.

I was shocked. Hanging out with the wrong crowds, going against my mom's wishes by having people over, and thinking I was "grown" because I was changing classes and going to school with handsome ninth graders led to a significant decline in my studies. I even tried to cut a two-period class during the start of the second period! Of course, I got caught. I still don't know what I was thinking. My mindset was completely off, so I had to get it together. I realized that I couldn't keep doing the same thing and expecting different results.

According to Einstein, that was insanity. I knew that faith was going to be a way I could get some of the answers I had been looking for, so I thought, perhaps, attending a different church would help. I started to attend the church my dad took me to a few times before, and that changed everything. I began taking the hour-long hike from Queens to Brooklyn each week to hear the word, and I started applying what I was learning.

That summer, I discovered how powerful words were in shaping my mind and how my mindset was affecting everything I did. I quickly got back to what I knew, began studying more, and surrounded myself with a crowd that also aimed to achieve high grades. Of course, I still hung out with people who knew how to have fun, but that wasn't their sole focus.

Understanding the Growth vs. Fixed Mindset

It's important to understand the difference between a *Growth Mindset* and a *Fixed Mindset*.

With a Fixed Mindset, you are limited, stuck on what's right in front of you. In contrast, a Growth Mindset helps you believe in what you can grow into beyond your current circumstances.

A person with a Growth Mindset views intelligence, abilities, and skills as things you can develop through effort over time. On the other hand, someone with a Fixed Mindset believes these talents are static and unchangeable.

You may have heard of a *Scarcity Mindset*, sometimes referred to as a *Poverty Mindset*. This mindset leads you to always think that resources will run out. While it's okay to be realistic and grounded in your thoughts, constantly believing there won't be enough for you can be limiting.

The *Scarcity Mindset* can also hold us back on our career paths, especially if we think everyone else is already doing what we want to do. But there are countless examples of people succeeding even in fields where there's already significant competition. Think of the water aisle in the supermarket. You see plenty of companies selling water. But just because there are several water brands doesn't stop an entrepreneur from launching their own. Why? This has happened repeatedly. New water brands enter a crowded market and still find success.

Think in terms of abundance, not lack. I'm not suggesting you spend money carelessly, but this is something to consider as you begin to set financial goals and pursue purpose. Even before you write down your goals, work on your mindset. Focus on growth, stay positive, and know that, though there may be competition, there's always room for you to thrive.

When I had a Fixed Mindset, I didn't take risks—something that is crucial for growth. If I hadn't shifted my mindset, I wouldn't have joined the coaching programs that I did, first with Marshawn Evans Daniels and then with Eric Thomas & Associates Game Changers. Though costly, those programs helped me grow in business, personal, and professional development.

From around 2015 to 2019, personal development became a major part of my life. It was so ingrained in me that I didn't just use it for myself—I started teaching these tools to the girls in my *Brown Girls GLOW* program, and I even brought that mindset to my job.

While working at *STEVE*, Steve Harvey's Emmy Award-winning talk show, I pitched an idea for a *Lunch & Learn* series, where the production assistants could ask questions and learn directly from the executive producers. I was nervous about speaking up, but the idea got approved! Before the season ended, we hosted a midday Q&A at Universal Studios with about 20 PAs and both EPs— veterans of the TV industry. That one event helped plant a seed.

Not long after, during Memorial Day Weekend, I noticed Steve Harvey was hosting the *Vault Empowers Summit*, a three-day professional development event. I reached out to someone I knew on his business team at Steve Harvey Global (SHG) and asked if I could volunteer. They said yes.

What I didn't know was that behind the scenes, they were looking to relaunch the *Act Like a Success, Think Like a Success* program— and they needed to hire a new manager to lead the effort.

An executive from the SHG team asked one of the executive producers from *STEVE* about me. My EP gave me a great review, and she told them about the professional development session I had just organized for the production assistants. That endorsement, combined with my already volunteering at the summit, made me stand out. Days later, I was offered the role.

At the time, I had just accepted the offer for a receptionist job at *Family Guy*—which would've meant a pay cut—but I almost took it because I wanted to do whatever it took to stay connected to the industry. Nonetheless, as God would have it, shortly thereafter, I was offered a managerial position that not only paid significantly more but also allowed me to stay in entertainment.

This all happened because I shifted my mindset.

Glitter Dust

As I mentioned in the first few lines of this chapter, *Mindset Determines Your Attitude. Attitude Determines Approach. Approach Determines Success or Failure.* This is a quote by Dr. A.R. Bernard. If you want to grow, you must first believe in your mind that you can. I always say that if you can see it, you can believe it, and if you believe it, you can achieve it. It might sound like something you learned in elementary school, but it's a principle I live by every day.

If you can see the lifestyle, career, school, or any goal you want to achieve, believe that you can get there, and you're one step closer to making it happen. This mindset will help you set goals and approach them with enthusiasm, which you'll need to stay consistent. The more you water your seeds and nurture them, the more they will grow.

Remember when I said I messed up in middle school? I had to use this mindset shift in eighth grade to work my way back into honors classes. I focused on schoolwork, made the honor roll, and even excelled on the basketball court. I attended church and youth groups regularly, too. By the end of the year, I had worked my way back into the honors program for ninth grade (my middle school went from seventh to ninth grade). I humbled myself, accepted the fact that I didn't know everything, and listened to my mom, mentors, and teachers.

Although I was focused and doing better in school in ninth grade, by tenth grade, high school presented a whole new world for me. With more students and more opportunities for self-esteem issues, high school presented challenges. I had to learn that a major part of having a healthy mindset is maintaining a healthy self-image.

Your Mindset Shapes Your Momentum

"Mindset determines your attitude. Attitude determines approach. Approach determines success or failure." – Dr. A.R. Bernard

If your mindset is the soil, your self-image is the seed. A seed won't grow without being nurtured. You have already seen how powerful your thoughts can be—now let's pause and reflect on how your internal narrative has shaped your path so far.

Reflections

1. Do you ever remember a time when you had a scarcity mindset?

2. How can having a growth mindset help you achieve your goals?

3. How can you improve your mindset?

3. Nurture Your Nature and Your Self Narrative

My mom has encouraged me to be more self-confident since I was a teenager. She always said I could be "cute, fly, and smart"—her way of saying she wanted me to have both style and substance. She emphasized the importance of putting your best foot forward when it came to your presentation, and she always reminded me that while I was beautiful, I should aim to be more than just a pretty face. Intelligence mattered.

As I mentioned earlier, my dominant temperament is Phlegmatic. We tend to be dependable, but unassertiveness is one of our weaknesses. Confidence definitely plays a role in helping us be more assertive, and a positive self-image is crucial for boosting that confidence.

In an article on PositivePsychology.com titled, *'What is Self-Image in Psychology? How Do We Improve It?'* the authors explain that self-image is how you perceive yourself—a mix of positive or negative self-impressions that build up over time. This can give someone confidence in their thoughts and actions or make them doubtful of their capabilities and ideas.

Learning that a better perception of myself could help boost my confidence motivated me to be kinder to myself. Maintaining a positive self-image has proven to be critical for my growth.

Here is another quote I want to share with you:

> *"Self-image sets the boundaries of individual accomplishment."*
> - Maxwell Maltz

In order to grow, we must expand our reach. We can't limit ourselves by having a negative self-image and believing that we can't accomplish something we're fully capable of doing. We may not be able to do something alone or do several things all at the same time; nonetheless, almost anything is possible.

Self-Image vs. Self-Esteem

Thinking highly of yourself must be accompanied by feeling good about yourself. That's the difference between self-image and self-esteem. Image relates to perception, while esteem is about our sense of respect for ourselves and how favorably (or unfavorably) we view ourselves.

Sporadically, a negative self-image may try to creep into my mindset, although over the years, I've learned to overcome negative thinking with positive words, affirmations, and prayer. Find what works best for you. It is said that it takes twelve good thoughts to counter one bad one, so make sure to speak about what you want rather than what you currently see.

For example, if you're struggling in a class, don't tell yourself, "This class is impossible to pass. I'll never be able to get an A." Say instead, "Though this class is challenging, I am up for the challenge and will do my very best to excel." Then, take action steps such as speaking to a student who is performing well in that class, asking the teacher for help and suggestions, and applying what you learn from them both to improve your study methods.

Comparison is the thief of joy. Don't let comparison rob you of your self-esteem by measuring your experiences or journey against someone else's. The only person you should compare yourself to is you. Who you were before vs. who you are now.

Celebrate your accomplishments and milestones each step of the way.

Another tip for maintaining a positive self-image is to read books that uplift you as a young woman, not just what the media and brands promote. Be intentional about what you consume, especially when you're feeling down or not at your best. That includes both what you eat and the content you engage with, whether online or offline.

There are eight forms of media, each telling you different things about what you should do and how you should feel about yourself. Be conscious of the traps and false narratives. Know that you were made the way you are for a reason.

Now I can suggest ways on how to maintain a healthy self-image, but I do remember a time in college when I started to worry about my weight. I was obsessively tracking my calorie intake and was constantly fighting with the scale. Thankfully, I found comfort in listening to Mary Mary's first album. There was one song in particular that I had on repeat, and it helped me build my self-confidence. It was called "*Little Girl*." It talked about struggling with confidence, loving yourself, shared affirmations, and God's promises.

My friend Aleea and I listened to that song all the time. Hearing it, along with meditating on scriptures that emphasized how God made me beautiful in His image, I was able to gain the confidence I needed to have a healthier outlook on my weight. I didn't focus on what I weighed as a measure of how healthy I was but what I ate and how I felt, making sure to incorporate rest and leisure into my busy college schedule.

This newfound confidence also encouraged me to choose a new major—Sport Management. It helped me decide to go to China to teach English for five weeks. I saw the flyer announcing the opportunity on the door at the Honors College office at Hampton University. I spent my twentieth birthday in orientation for the school in Hangzhou, where I would be teaching. It was mesmerizing having an auditorium full of students singing happy birthday to me. They even gave me a cake!

Glitter Dust

Don't compare yourself to others, especially their highlight reel. You cannot see the full picture of someone else's life on social media. Be your best and healthiest self, knowing that you are beautiful no matter how different you may look from society's standards.

My mom's mantra for me—to be "cute, fly, and smart"—has stuck with me. She used to remind me of it when she saw me with my head down or with a melancholy demeanor when it came to something I was working on. She said it because, in most cases, the media portrays the idea that you can only be beautiful *or* intellectual. But know that you can be both. You are intelligent and gifted in ways that are uniquely yours.

You may have heard the phrase "book smart" vs. being smart in other areas (i.e., street smart). Know that you can be knowledgeable in any area, not just in books. There's something that you know more than others, and that makes you unique. You can use that knowledge to fulfill your biggest dreams and goals.

Once you develop a healthier self-image, you'll find that you can be more disciplined and stick to the things that will help you achieve your biggest goals. This growth will benefit not only you but your community as well.

Glow From the Inside Out

Let's reflect on what's fueling your inner light—and what might be dimming it.

1. Can you recall a moment when a negative self-image held you back? What would you do differently now?

2. If "self-image sets the boundaries of individual accomplishment," what boundaries might you be placing on yourself because of how you see yourself?

3. What three things can you do to improve your self-image?

4. What would it look like for you to embrace your version of health, confidence, and success?

Part 2

LEAD

4. The Power of Discipline

When I think of discipline, I think of the time I became intentional about my schedule as a college student. Thankfully, when I shared that I was overwhelmed with my classwork with my mentor Pastor Roslyn, she gave me a tool to help me become more disciplined and strategic with my weekly schedule.

GLOW GIRL SCHEDULE
SAMPLE TEMPLATE

TIME	MON	TUE	WED	THU	FRI	SAT	SUN
6:00							
7:00							
8:00							
9:00							
10:00							
11:00							
12:00							
1:00							
2:00							
3:00							
4:00							
5:00							
6:00							
7:00							
8:00							
9:00							
10:00							

GLOW GIRL SCHEDULE TEMPLATE
*SAMPLE

TIME	MON	TUE	WED	THU	FRI	SAT	SUN
6:00		GYM		GYM			
7:00							
8:00				LIT 101		HIKE	
9:00	MATH			LIT 101			GROWTH
10:00	MATH					CLEAN ROOM	GROWTH
11:00		BIO			UNI 101		
12:00	LUNCH	BIO	STUDENT COUNCIL				LEISURE
1:00		LUNCH	LUNCH				
2:00							PLAN
3:00		STUDY		PHYS ED			PLAN
4:00		STUDY	STUDY	PHYS ED	WORK STUDY		
5:00			STUDY		WORK STUDY		
6:00	DINNER		DINNER				
7:00			BAND	DANCE CLASS		REST	
8:00			BAND			FUN	
9:00						FUN	
10:00	SLEEP	SLEEP		SLEEP			

She asked me to assign my classes to specific time slots. I also included time for lunch, breaks, Bible study, church, exercise, and hanging out with friends. This shift helped me improve both my grades and my peace of mind. Having set study times encouraged me to stick to a routine that helped me excel, especially with my tendency to be indecisive. I believe keeping that schedule prepared me for the journey that led to my acceptance to and graduation from Harvard.

On another occasion, on a typical Sunday, the summer before my final year at Hampton University, I was sitting in a church service at Christian Cultural Center. Dr. Bernard was making announcements about what was happening in the community and informing the congregation about an available scholarship. Believers who were thinking of attending one of the top schools in their desired graduate school major were encouraged to apply to The Harvey Fellowship.

Since I was actively looking for funding to go to graduate school, I paid close attention to the details. After church, I found my dad, who was serving in the church parking lot, and spoke with him about the announcement and the opportunity for a scholarship.

"What if I went to Yale or Princeton or someplace like that?" I asked him.

We both actually thought it was funny, but there was a side of it where we knew that only God could make it happen. We spoke about how I grew up in the Projects, less than 15 minutes away from our church. Yet I was thinking about applying to an Ivy League school. The audacity! Nonetheless, I did what I always have done before I made a big decision: I prayed about it.

I started conducting some research, leaving Harvard till the last one to review. I thought Harvard would be the most expensive and the hardest to get into. My research showed me that graduate programs in education at the other Ivy League schools didn't have majors that spoke to the work and research in which I was interested.

Lo and behold, when I went to Harvard's Graduate School of Education site, I found a program that spoke directly to what I wanted to dive into, such as education in informal learning environments and using nontraditional methods. By the time I got back to campus in Virginia, I felt God speaking to me, letting me know that He would be working through me to ultimately "glow" in graduate school. With that charge, I worked tirelessly on my application, turned it in, and, four months later, was admitted.

I tell this story to show you what is possible through discipline. Before you can lead others, you first have to be effective at leading yourself. Discipline enables you to lead yourself. It is the bridge between a goal and its accomplishment.

You can become the best version of yourself through discipline. We become what we do repeatedly.

What can you do each day to become your best self?

Here are five habits that can help you prepare for leadership. You don't have to try to implement all of these at once, and you may already be incorporating some. Do what works best for you.

1. **Get a morning routine.**
   This could include prayer, meditation, or anything that centers you before the day gets busy. Be intentional.

2. **Keep your living and workspace organized.**
   Having a system in place will make it easier to find what you need. This doesn't have to cost much but will require some time and effort. There are tons of resources, especially on YouTube, to help you organize. Find a system that works for you. Your version of an organized space might look different from someone else's, and that's okay.

3. **Exercise.**
   This applies to your body and your mind. You don't have to walk 10,000 steps a day, and maybe you're not in a place where you can move your body much, but getting your blood flowing—even if it's just for a few minutes each day—has been proven to have a positive impact on both your physical and mental health. Also, reading books, whether fiction or nonfiction, will help you to exercise your mind.

4. **Work toward your goals.**
   If you haven't set any goals yet, now is the time to start. These can be physical, mental, emotional, spiritual, academic, career, personal, or any other type of goals you can imagine.

5. **Set an evening routine.**
   Some say that the next day begins the night before. If you list your priorities and set your schedule before going to sleep, your mind will have time to process those thoughts and plans, helping you execute them the next day.

For much of my childhood, I was very active. I took dance classes and competed in dance competitions from the age of three to the age of twelve. I stopped dancing with a company at twelve because my school didn't offer a free dance program, and we couldn't afford the paid classes at the time. I'd like to give a shoutout to the *East New York Theatrical Workshop*, which offered classes to children from the Projects and gave them opportunities to perform around the city.

When I moved to Queens, my school had a dance program led by our teacher at P.S. 164, Mr. Dobbs, and I was able to continue my passion for dance. We had some of the best times!

But when I got to middle school at Russell Sage, the school didn't offer dance, although they had drama, Latin, and other extracurricular classes, including basketball.

I participated in Drama, choosing it as an elective in both seventh and ninth grades (I chose Latin in eighth grade - which greatly helped with my vocabulary), but I also wanted to do something more physically active. Dancing, basketball, and other sports taught me that the more I practiced, the better I performed. I had to be disciplined to keep myself in shape, eat the right foods, and maintain an optimistic mindset to excel on the court and the stage. Getting involved in any active sport or activity helps build the muscle of discipline. If you continue to practice, the discipline will stay with you and positively impact other areas of your life.

Glitter Dust

Remember, *discipline is the bridge between a goal and its accomplishment*. I know you have big goals, and it will take discipline to achieve them. Build habits that will shape you into the person you want to be. We are what we do repeatedly.

My schedule led me to succeed in my classes and to prepare for graduate school. When I applied to Harvard, I knew I had to stick to a schedule to submit a stellar application, including an impactful personal essay. I went through seven versions of my essay, as I knew that the number seven symbolized completion. Thanks to my schedule grid, I was able to carve out time to work on my application during my third and final year at Hampton. By then, I had a rhythm for balancing study, work, and play. Once I submitted my application, I returned to focusing on my studies, and a year later, I matriculated at Harvard's Graduate School of Education.

If discipline was the bridge that got me to Harvard, then my friend circle and my "village" provided the fuel to get me across. When I began applying to Harvard, I had the opportunity to attend an in-person information session specifically for students of color in Cambridge, Massachusetts. I wasn't sure how I'd afford to stay in the Boston area, but when I told my friend Jackie Raye—a fellow Hampton student originally from Boston—she immediately connected me with her church family. They welcomed me with open arms, and I stayed with them for one night. That short visit made a huge difference: I was able to see the campus for the first time, learn more about the school, and meet Dr. Sally Schwager—who would later become my department head and one of my favorite professors. Having the right people around you— people who believe in you, advocate for you, and open doors—is essential to walking on purpose. And just as important is being that support for others too.

Discipline is the Daily Decision to Honor Your Dreams.

Before you lead others, you have to lead yourself. Let's reflect on how your habits shape your future.

1. What does "discipline" mean to you personally? How has your definition evolved over time?

2. Can you recall a time when a lack of discipline cost you something important?

3. How intentional are you with your current daily or weekly schedule?

4. Think about a dream school, job, or opportunity that feels too big. What daily or weekly habits can you begin (or continue) that will help you get closer to that goal?

5. How can being more disciplined help you become a better leader of yourself, in your school, family, or community?

5. Who's in Your Circle?

Positive peer pressure was my saving grace in high school and college. I'm incredibly thankful for the friends I met in *The Group*—my tribe in high school—and the *Fab Five*, my closest confidantes in college.

In high school, students were placed in tracks or groups based on similar test scores and reading levels. I was in honors classes, mostly with the same students every period. On my first day of high school, I was one of the new students because I transferred in as a sophomore, while most of my classmates had already been there for a year.

At the end of the school day, one of my classmates came up to me and asked if I had gone to P.S. 224, the school across the street from my grandmother's home. I said yes, and she told me she had attended there as well. It was Dawnelle, also known as "China," who had been my best friend in pre-kindergarten and kindergarten! We had lost touch after I was bussed to another school, and she had moved out of the neighborhood. But all these years later, we ended up in the same high school, in a completely different part of Brooklyn, yet in the same class!

Her friends were so cool. There was Tamika, our high school's valedictorian, who lived across the street from me; Shaulette, the mom of my only godchild, Omar, who played a role in my most recent short film; and Sam, who graduated third in our class and now lives in the same city as me. They all earned good grades and also knew how to have fun. That was one of the reasons we got along so well—they weren't trying to slack off from the honor roll, and they all wanted to make their families proud. They encouraged me to join clubs and excel, and I did because I didn't want to be left behind.

In college at Hampton University, the same thing happened. The *Fab Five*—Aleea, Chivon, Ebi, Atiya, and I—formed study groups, but we also prayed together and held each other accountable for our academic and personal goals. Over the years, we've stayed in touch. While some of our relationships have changed, we all still cherish the memories we created together.

Zig Ziglar says, "You are the average of the five people you hang out with the most." This principle—that who you surround yourself with impacts your lifestyle—dates all the way back to Biblical times. Proverbs 5:9 reminds us that bad company corrupts good character. You may have heard the saying, "Birds of a feather flock together." There are countless expressions warning us about the power of the company we keep. Who you spend time with will significantly affect your outcomes, so it's essential to surround yourself with people who challenge you, have a positive mindset, and encourage you to take care of yourself and live up to your fullest potential.

Now, I'm not saying that if you live or go to school with someone who doesn't have a positive attitude or doesn't get good grades, you should never interact with them or avoid them completely. It just means that if you want to achieve your goals, they may not be the best person to spend your time with. There's also a saying: "If you're the smartest person in your group, get a new group." This doesn't mean you should only hang out with people smarter than you, but it suggests that it's beneficial to spend time with those who have insights into areas you may want to learn about. For example, you may be the most knowledgeable in your group on one topic, but a friend might be an expert in another area. Use your best judgment when choosing who to associate with because the people around you can help shape who you become.

Glitter Dust

Your Network: Relationships You Will Need to Succeed

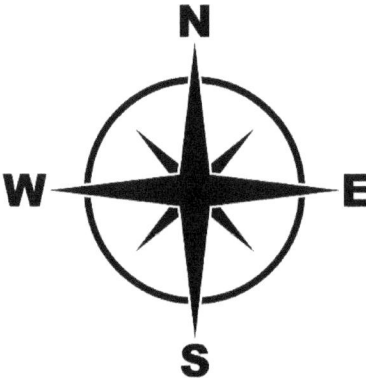

A compass is a tool used in navigation, usually to help direct one to where they need to go. When you are attending an event or thinking of a relationship, also consider the 'Relationship Compass':

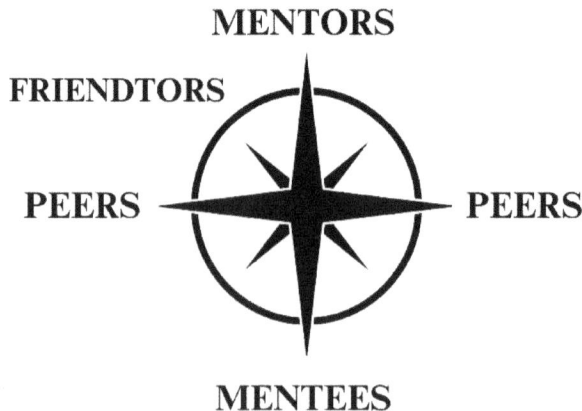

North, East, West, South: The Power of Relationships in Your Journey

North: When you think of the North, think about traveling 'up.' This is where your mentors, coaches, teachers, youth pastors, group leaders, and even your big brother or big sister come into play. These relationships include those who have succeeded in areas you'd like to accomplish and can help you get there—possibly faster—by helping you avoid the mistakes they made or by offering lessons they've learned along the way.

For example, my mentor, Karin Buchholz, was the first person who suggested I look in the *Yellow Pages* to find the top person in my dream industry or role and ask if I can take them to lunch. For those of you who remember, the Yellow Pages were how we found people's contact information before the internet. Now, websites like LinkedIn allow you to easily find individuals in positions you may not have even considered. Karin's advice was simple—if the top person doesn't respond, move on to the next. Keep going until you find someone willing to give you their time. And don't be afraid to reach out for a virtual coffee via platforms like Zoom or Google Meet, as the world of mentorship has evolved.

It's also important to remember that mentors don't always have to be people you meet in person. In his book, *10 Hollywood Commandments*, Devon Franklin talks about virtual mentors or "mentors in your head." These are people you follow online who give insight into your goals through interviews, podcasts, books, and more. Some of my virtual mentors in film include Gina Prince-Bythewood, Ava DuVernay, Issa Rae, Courtney Kemp, Mara Brock Akil, Tabitha Brown, Lena Waithe, and Will Packer. Whenever they have interviews available online, I listen closely, always searching for clues on how I, too, can thrive as a storyteller.

East and West: For this one, think of relationships with people on the same level as you. These could be peers, classmates, or others you meet who can collaborate with you or hold you accountable for the goals you set. Accountability partners are some of the most crucial people in your journey. There's an old saying that goes, "If you want to go fast, go alone. If you want to go far, go together." This perfectly illustrates the importance of surrounding yourself with people who can keep you accountable and motivate you to push toward your goals.

Amy Aniobi touches on a phrase, made viral by Issa Rae, called *networking across*—the idea that while many people seek guidance from those who have already achieved success, people who are on the same journey as you can be just as valuable in helping you 'glow up' to your next level. They understand the challenges you're facing and can share resources and experiences that could be the key to your next big achievement.

Further, some of your peers can also be your mentors and vice versa. When my friend is also my mentor, I call them my 'Friendtors, ' a phrase I learned from my friends Adena and Gabi G.

South: Going South on the relationship compass means giving back to those who may not be as far along as you are in their journey. This can be a powerful way to make an impact. Even if you're a teenager, you can contribute to your community. For instance, if you're a part of a team that works with multiple age groups, you can help coach or mentor younger players. Or you can advocate for those who may not have access to the same resources as yourself

Marley Dias was just eleven years old when she launched the #1000BlackGirlBooks campaign because she didn't see Black girl protagonists in her school's reading lists. She wanted to make sure young women had access to books with Black women protagonists. Through her campaign, with support from the GrassROOTS Community Foundation, she has since collected over 15,000 books!

Remember, even when you're at the beginning stages of your journey, there are always opportunities to give back. You have a gift, not just for yourself but to help make the world a better place—even if it's only one person at a time.

Coming from a family where I was a first-generation college graduate, I am grateful for the mentors I met through PowerPlay, NYC. Some of these mentors were also first-generation college students. Others, such as the founder, Dr. Ellen Markowitz, had multiple generations of college graduates. When I was applying to Harvard, Ellen helped me with my personal essay. She was the only person I knew personally who had gone to an Ivy League school, and I knew her insights would be invaluable. I remember sitting in the PowerPlay office, where she gave me feedback on the final draft of my essay before I submitted my application. I'll forever be grateful for her guidance.

I also owe a lot of my achievements to other mentors like Karin Buchholz and Mr. Alfred Edmond, Jr. Karin and I first connected when I was a counselor at PowerPlay's STARS Summer Leadership Academy. I met her when we took students on a trip to visit the New York Knicks' corporate offices. Karin, who came from a low-income background, became a mentor of mine. I stayed in touch with her for two years before she helped me secure an internship with the Knicks during my last year at Hampton University.

Alfred Edmond, Jr. and I crossed paths during a Business Plan Pitch Competition for young entrepreneurs, where I won a prize for my business, Phenomenon Education Services.

Alfred taught me an essential principle that has stuck with me over the years: "Mentorship is not owed, it is earned." This idea was the subject of an article he wrote for Black Enterprise, where he emphasized that mentors often choose mentees based on their willingness to work hard and give back. As I sought to help Mr. Edmond, he encouraged me to "pay it forward" or "pass the baton"—a phrase borrowed from a powerful book on mentorship by Bishop Dale Bronner. Over the twenty-plus years I've known him, Mr. Edmond has provided me with countless opportunities, including my first chance to write professionally, job recommendations, and advice. It was my pleasure to volunteer and show up for his events and projects whenever I could.

The principle that Devon Franklin shares—*"Carry a crown before you wear one"*—perfectly encapsulates how you should approach relationships in your journey. Serve others, support your mentors, and be willing to give back in meaningful ways.

I am immensely thankful for the peer groups and mentors who have inspired and supported me throughout my life. Their practice of giving back to others has been a significant factor in their success, and I've followed their example throughout my journey.

Let's Talk About *You* ...

Reading about someone else's journey is powerful—but what matters most is your own. Ready to explore?

1. Who are the five people you spend the most time with? How do they influence your goals, habits, and mindset?

2. Can you identify any relationships that push you to be your best self? What makes them so impactful?

3. Have you ever had a virtual mentor? Who are they? What have you learned from them?

4. What's one thing you could do this week to strengthen a mentor or peer relationship?

5. How can you carry a crown before you wear one on your own journey?

Glow Girl

Glow Girl. Shine from the inside out.
Do not be defined by filters or followers

but by faith, focus, and fire.

Choose confidence over comparison.
Compassion over competition.
Purpose over perfection.

Don't wait for permission to glow—
know your light was meant to be seen.

Learn, lead, and lift others as you climb.
Reflect the beauty of bold dreams
and the power of believing in yourself.

This is your invitation
to become who you were always meant to be.

6. Shining Through Service

C ommunity service has been a cornerstone of my personal and professional growth. During high school, I actively participated in a variety of organizations and nonprofits that offered free programming. Today, whether at church or through institutions like the National Urban League or the NAACP, I continue to volunteer for or serve through these programs—not only to give back but also to build relationships, hone my skills, and broaden my network.

PowerPlay, NYC offered a free after-school program that I attended in high school. After my freshman year in college, I worked there over the summer. When I graduated from Harvard, it was challenging for me to secure a full-time role. PowerPlay only had enough funding to hire me on a part-time basis as a program coordinator, but I gladly worked in the role because I knew it would give me experience in an area in which I was interested. I enjoyed making an impact on young women who were like me a few years earlier. The days that I was not at PowerPlay gave me the opportunity to intern for a film called *Brooklyn to Manhattan*, directed by Jesse Terrero.

At PowerPlay, I assisted with programs, fundraising, and coaching girls throughout the city. After about six months, we hosted our first major luncheon at Grand Central Terminal in New York City. It was a beautiful setup. My manager, Beth Rasin, as well as Ellen, wanted me to speak about my experience as a past participant. I recalled that my mentor, Karin Buchholz, told me that each job she obtained after retiring from professional tennis was secured as a result of someone hearing her speak. I was still looking for a full-time role then, and I told myself, "I need to work hard on this speech so that someone can hear me and offer me a first full-time position."

Leading up to the event, I outlined and practiced my speech. I even read it to Beth, who had known me since I started as a participant at sixteen years old. When it was my turn to speak, Ms. Beth introduced me. She said that as much as she'd love to hire me full time, she couldn't because of budgetary restraints, which was why they were having the fundraiser. I went up to speak with confidence and energy. As I said, I needed to get a role out of this. I didn't know where it would come from or if it would come at all, but I wanted to give my best. I spoke about how PowerPlay taught me to dream big, take my education seriously, and find a mentor to help me achieve my goals.

Once I got off the stage, Beth introduced Donna Orender, the President of the WNBA at the time. The first thing Donna said was, "Anyone who can speak like that about their organization should be on my team. Mia, I want you to come work with me!"

I was in shock! The crowd started clapping, and all I could say was—*thank you!* She told me who to contact to work out the logistics, and the rest was history. I received an offer for my first role with a major corporation after completing graduate school, which was with the WNBA.

Volunteering your time or serving with an organization you're passionate about can help you discover what you enjoy or dislike before committing to a career or academic path. Even in college or once you're established in your career, offering your help can allow you to explore a new field, network, learn more about a specific industry, or make the changes you desire.

Glitter Dust

Giving back benefits both you and the community you serve. Some of the advantages of volunteering for community organizations include:

- Networking with professionals in the industry who are often eager to share their experiences with you
- Accessing events or conferences at no cost
- Gaining valuable skills and work experience to enhance your resume for future paid positions

I vividly remember Mr. Edmond telling me about Black Enterprise's Women of Power Summit. At this annual event, top Black women executives and major brands from across the country come together to learn, network, and foster a sense of community. At that time, as a college student, I was eager to attend but lacked the financial means to purchase a ticket. So, I approached Mr. Edmond about volunteering, and he graciously connected me with the team. That was how I was able to attend. Although I covered my airfare and hotel costs, the savings on the ticket made it possible for me to 'be in the room.'

The experience was unforgettable. It was my first time attending such a large conference for working professionals, and working behind the scenes to help make it happen was both thrilling and inspiring. One of the highlights was meeting the many incredible women in attendance. I recall that during the conference, I was on the team that placed a copy of the current month's Black Enterprise magazine in the gift bags. The cover featured a stunning woman who was also a keynote speaker, Joi Gordon. I had the chance to hear her speak and, by chance, encountered her in the elevator afterward.

I introduced myself and congratulated her on her cover story. She graciously thanked me and then asked where I was from. When I told her New York, she smiled and said, "I'll see you back in New York then." I was thrilled. Joi was someone I deeply admired as a mom, wife, and the CEO of a nonprofit dedicated to supporting unemployed and underemployed women to achieve economic independence and thrive in work and life—Dress for Success. This passion of hers resonated with me deeply, as empowering women has always been a passion of mine as well. She took me on as a mentee, and we stayed in touch for years. The advice she offered me was invaluable, and I am forever grateful.

To accomplish things you've never done, you must venture into places you've never been, which may include industry events you're interested in. Even if you can't afford the ticket, volunteering is a great way to gain access, especially when you're younger.

As Muhammad Ali once said, community service is how you "pay rent for your time on Earth." Not only will you learn about your chosen career, but you'll also contribute to the betterment of your community. I'm thankful for those who've chosen to give back to others who were once in similar circumstances. Many of them were the first in their families to have the opportunity to pursue their dreams, and they want to ensure they support students who face similar challenges.

Now It's Your Turn to Make a Difference...

You've read how showing up to serve changed my life. What could happen if you showed up too?

1. What causes or communities are you passionate about serving? Why do they matter to you?

2. Have you ever discovered a new interest or skill through service work? What was the experience like?

3. What's one example of a time you gave your best, even without a guaranteed reward or recognition?

4. How might volunteering or community service help you grow in your career or education?

5. In what ways can you pay rent for your time on earth right now—even if it's something small?

PART 3
OVERCOME

7. First-Generation Flame

My grandmother, Leona Hall, called Noni by her family and who never graduated from high school, had the joy of seeing me walk across the stage at Harvard with my master's degree when she was eighty-one years old. She once shared with me, in a report I wrote about her for one of my Women's History classes at Harvard, that she had left high school to work and help support her family. As the eldest of five children, she took on the responsibility of helping her mom cover their family's expenses. Despite their modest circumstances, she managed to keep what seemed like hundreds of books in our two-bedroom project apartment. She told me she had gotten those books from a woman whose house she used to clean. According to her, the woman didn't make her work much; instead, she let her read for most of her time there. The books in our house were some that the woman had allowed my grandmother to take home.

I share this story because it mirrors the experiences of many elders in undervalued communities. Until 1867, it was illegal for enslaved and sometimes free Black Americans to read or write. This historical context is crucial for understanding why, even in 2025, many people still face the reality of being first-generation college students. Due to the lasting effects of racism, white supremacy, and numerous other systemic barriers, people of color have been denied some of the same opportunities as their white counterparts. Yet, this is far from the end of their story. As we have witnessed countless times, people of color continue to blaze trails for their communities—both on a national level and within their families.

Although no one in my immediate family had graduated from college by the time I attended Hampton University, they equipped me with everything I needed to succeed. They sparked my first-generation flame. They taught me how to be resourceful, encouraged my involvement in the arts, and affirmed that I could achieve anything if I believed I could and worked hard enough.

The first time I got to experience being on a college campus was when my dad was a student at Hunter College in New York City. He ran for the school's track team and stayed in the dorms at twenty-nine years old. He used to bring my sister Jhanee and my godsisters Tiffany, Rhonda, and Charisma on the train to visit the school and see what it was like. He only left because his friend, Mike Tyson, called him to start working on his team again. From then on, my dad would be on the road with Mike for every fight, and sometimes, the New Breed— what my dad called his godchildren that he would take out— would travel with him.

Though my dad had to leave school, he taught my sisters and his godchildren all he could about life. He would always bring us to Manhattan to see the tree at Rockefeller Center during the Christmas season, public performances at Times Square, ice skating in Central Park, to the Empire State Building, and more. Though we didn't live in the same household, he did what he could to expose me, my sister, and the New Breed to anything he could outside of the Projects, which was an education within itself.

Understand that everything you have learned, no matter where you come from, will serve you as you navigate specific spaces that may be unfamiliar to those around you.

Glitter Dust

Tips for First-Generation College Students:

- Take full advantage of the free resources available to you.
- Surround yourself with mentors who can guide you through experiences your family may not be familiar with, such as navigating the college and scholarship application processes.
- Recognize that both you and your family possess unique skill sets that will serve you in school and beyond.

I remember spending countless hours in my high school's college counselor, Ms. Valentine's, office while applying for colleges. Although my parents both attended college, neither of them finished before I entered high school. My mom attended Morgan State University for a semester but had to leave to care for me. And like I said, I visited my dad's campus where he went for two years, but he left to take a once-in-a-lifetime opportunity to work with one of the world's heavyweight champions. This left me to rely on Ms. Valentine and my village of teachers and mentors to guide me through the college application process. My English teacher, Ms. Gentile, was one of my favorites and played a crucial role in helping me craft strong essays and personal statements.

During my senior year, I also worked at an after-school program, where, ironically, four of my coworkers had recently graduated from Hampton University. When they found out I was undecided on where I would go to school, they heavily insisted on their beloved alma mater. They encouraged me throughout the application process.

Through this same job, my supervisor, Oma Holloway, introduced me to a program called APEX, which held bi-weekly college prep classes led by Brother Carlos Walton, also a Hampton alum. While participating in APEX, I had the opportunity to attend a Historically Black College and University (HBCU) tour, which included visits to Hampton University and several other campuses. In addition to touring campuses, we learned about Black history facts I had never heard of in grade school. We watched movies like *Sankofa*, which deepened my understanding of my history and the significance of HBCUs in our society.

Know this: you possess a unique and valuable set of skills, regardless of whether your family attended college.

As you pursue your goals, you may not have anyone in your immediate circle to share stories of their own "ups and downs" on similar paths. However, remember that 1) your family's experiences may still offer valuable insights, and 2) others have walked similar paths and are willing to share their journeys with you. Don't be afraid to ask for help.

Even if you are the first in your family or community to pursue a particular goal, ensure you aren't the last. If you approach your journey with purpose, you will blaze a trail that others will not only walk but also run on.

Your Journey Is a Legacy in the Making...

You may be the first in your family to walk this path—but you're opening doors for generations to come.

1. In what ways has your family's story sparked the fire that drives you today?

2. What lessons have you learned outside the classroom that have helped you succeed in school or life?

3. Think of a time you felt out of place or unsure in a new environment. What helped you adjust, succeed, or keep going?

4. What steps can you take now to find (or become) a mentor who understands your (or your mentees) journey?

5. What's one resource, tip, or truth that helped you— and could help someone else succeed?

8. Shine with What You Steward

Stewardship - the conducting, supervising, or managing of something; especially the careful and responsible management of something entrusted to one's care.

When I was a teenager, I didn't have a lot of money—but I was learning how to manage and be a good steward over what I had. I remember the first time I gave ten percent of my babysitting earnings to my church. I had six dollars and felt led to give. After service, I happened to run into my Uncle Diz, who handed me twelve dollars—without knowing what I had just given. That moment stuck with me. It wasn't just about the money. It was about learning that when you take good care of what you've been given—your time, your gifts, your money—God has a way of multiplying it. The next week, I gave an obscure amount again, and somehow, my mom's friend, whom I used to babysit for, gave me double what I gave as well. It happened at least three other times from what I remember. A true testimony.

I'm thankful that in college, *Rich Dad, Poor Dad* was on the required reading list for a finance class I was taking. It taught me that, often, people with financial wealth have a different mindset from those who aren't financially independent. Before reading that book, I understood the importance of managing my finances, but I didn't know how to grow them. I've always been committed to giving ten percent of my earnings to ministry efforts, and I've seen that money come back to me in unexpected ways. However, reading books on personal finance gave me the context and mindset I needed to build and maintain a healthy relationship with money.

For context, mindset is certainly not the only factor influencing financial freedom, especially among specific demographics. Systems like redlining (a discriminatory housing practice that once marked Black neighborhoods as high-risk and denied them loans), the prison-industrial complex, and the criminalization of undervalued groups have all created deep barriers. Still, this section focuses on mindset—the tool many have used to build wealth even when starting with limited resources.

I'm sharing this now because I wish someone had talked to me about money when I was a teenager. I didn't learn much about it in school or even at home, but it affects nearly every part of your life. That's why I wanted to include it in this guide. If you want to grow in this area, start reading books by financial experts. A few who have really shaped my thinking are Jacquette Timmons (who mentored me after college), Rachel Rodgers, and Tiffany "The Budgetnista" Aliche.

Like so many things in life, how you manage the money you have now prepares you for what's next. If you can learn to earn, give, save, budget, and invest wisely—even in small amounts— you'll be ready to handle more when the time comes. The financial habits you build today will set the stage for the rewards you'll see later.

When I was about twenty-four years old, Jacquette became my financial advisor for a year through my mentor, Diane King Hall. She and I met quarterly and checked in regularly. Through Jacquette, I learned the importance of budgeting, maintaining a savings account, and understanding various investment options for my future. Developing healthy financial habits early in my career has allowed me to take control of my finances and monitor them effectively.

Choosing a Career for the Money

While working in education, I still wanted to earn more money. I recall speaking with my mentor, Keith White, Esq, about my desire to attend law school or pursue a field that offered better financial rewards so I could achieve greater economic freedom. He told me something I still share with those just starting their careers: *"Don't choose a career just because it will make you rich. Choose something you're good at or skilled in and get rich at it."*

Now, a disclaimer—even though I'm not there yet financially, what I've learned has empowered me to glow up from the inside out—and that's something money can't buy.

I enjoy a rich life. I, fortunately, never had to file for bankruptcy. Still, I've found myself in some challenging financial situations by choosing paths that didn't promise the highest economic returns. If you read the stories of some of the biggest names in our society, many of them have faced financial hardships at one time. Nonetheless, being intentional and responsible with the finances you've earned or have been entrusted with will reap generous rewards.

At the time I spoke with my mentor, I thought staying in education would eventually bring me the financial rewards I desired. However, I've come to realize that the wealth I was seeking was not just economic—it was also wealth in well-being. Wanting support in taking my next most meaningful steps, I invested in a Dream Development coach for guidance. Sonya White, whom I met while still in graduate school, led me through a powerful process that helped me evaluate a few different career paths—education (specifically running my education services firm), sports, and film. I ultimately chose to begin in sports, where I was able to thrive, using my full skill set and building a strong foundation for my professional journey.

Investing in yourself is one of the best investments you can make. I began learning about finances in college, and since then, I've continued to study how to be a good steward of my money. Seek advice from certified financial experts and those with experience in building wealth. Don't listen to someone who has not built the kind of wealth you desire. Additionally, learn the basics of legacy planning and generational wealth for your family.

Glitter Dust

Seven Tips for Building a Healthy Financial Foundation in High School

1. Practice a positive growth mindset towards finances.
2. Learn about financial management for teens by reading books on the subject.
3. If you've never done it, try giving 10% of your after-school or business earnings to your place of faith or a charity that you like to support and observe the outcomes.
4. Track your spending, even if just for a set period.
5. Create and stick to a budget, even if just for a set period.
6. Listen to podcasts and watch YouTube videos from financial experts.

7. Remember that money is a means to an end, not the end itself. There are legal ways to get what you need without money.

No matter how much you earn, living with purpose will keep you going when you feel like giving up. Knowing that you're working for something bigger than yourself will keep you motivated through life's inevitable challenges.

Wealth Is More Than Money

What you manage today prepares you for the blessings of tomorrow.

1. When you hear the word *wealth*, what comes to mind—money, freedom, impact, or something else?

2. Do you believe you can live a rich life, even before you're financially wealthy? Why or why not?

3. What are your spending patterns when you're feeling emotional—bored, sad, or celebratory?

4. Have you ever created a budget? If not, what's held you back? If yes, what worked and what didn't?

5. Have you ever given to a cause or person and seen the return in unexpected ways? What did you learn from that experience?

9. Fuel the Flame – Living by Purpose

If the purpose of a thing is misunderstood, abuse is inevitable.

When I was sixteen, I thought I understood what it meant to have a purpose. I was active in church, reading the Bible regularly in high school, and I frequently heard, "God loves you and has a purpose for your life." But honestly, it always felt distant, like something I'd figure out when I was older. Then, during my senior year of high school, everything changed.

My supervisor, Ms. Holloway, introduced me to a program called ACRES, which stood for *American Civil Rights Education Services*. As a student always interested in history, I eagerly signed up. We had bi-weekly classes and learned about many crucial details of the Civil Rights Movement. My instructor, the late Sean Devlin, taught us far more than I ever learned in school about this topic.

Toward the end of the school year, we went on a tour of key Civil Rights landmarks in the South. We visited at least nine significant sites where courageous people fought for equality, and we spoke with visionaries like David Dennis in Birmingham, Alabama, James Meredith in Mississippi, and Diane Bland in Selma, Alabama.

All the stops were meaningful, but the one that stayed with me was Little Rock, Arkansas. There, we met Elizabeth Eckford, one of the Little Rock Nine. She shared her story, and it wasn't just a history lesson—it was her life.

I'll never forget how she described the experience of integrating Little Rock Central High School. She told us that every morning, she walked to school with a change of clothes in her bag. By midday, her clothes would be soaked with spit from people who teased her for simply going to school. She said she could ring out the saliva from her dress with her hands.

I was stunned. Sitting there listening to Ms. Eckford, I felt a deep sadness in my chest. I had heard about the Civil Rights Movement before, but hearing her story firsthand brought those sacrifices into sharp focus. She was just a teenager, like me. Still, she faced humiliation daily, not only for herself but also for those who would follow her in the fight for an equal education.

That moment changed me. It wasn't just about feeling inspired—it was as if a light switch flipped in my mind. Suddenly, "purpose" was no longer an abstract idea. It became real. I realized that I had to take my education seriously—not just for me but to honor the sacrifices made by people like Ms. Eckford, who fought for my opportunities as a scholar and Black woman.

What is Purpose?

For the context of this book, my definition of purpose is the reason you were brought into this world. I believe everyone has one. I recall reading Rick Warren's book *The Purpose-Driven Life* in my twenties. In it, Warren discusses living life with intention, grounded in biblical principles. It was incredibly helpful for me because I knew that living purposefully was a common trait of the people I admired. They talked about setting goals and pursuing them intentionally. They didn't go through life letting things happen to them or chasing after something just because it was popular or would make them a lot of money. That's what living a purposeful life entails.

I wanted to emphasize purpose because we are all born with one, and discovering it can dramatically shape the trajectory of our lives. Each of us is here to solve a specific problem, and we're uniquely gifted to do so. It's up to us to hone those gifts and refine them into skills that we can use to make a meaningful impact.

I also don't believe we have just one purpose. I don't think that once you discover one of your purposes, it will remain static. The purpose is something we continually unravel as we grow throughout our life's journey. It's not a finite answer but one that evolves as we emerge.

The reason I began this book discussing temperaments is so you can reflect on aspects of yourself that can help identify your unique gifts.

In this season of my life—not necessarily in accordance with the weather—I believe my purpose is to share what I've learned with young women so they can learn from my journey and map out their own paths. I am a storyteller who uplifts and inspires others through my words. I have more purposes, but these are especially important to me at this time.

Glitter Dust

Your purpose isn't just one thing; it progresses as you move along your journey.

One way to begin identifying your purpose is to use the "TIGER" method, which I learned about in college. I used it to consider my next steps after graduation.

T - Talent: *"What do people often compliment you on?"*

Talents are skills or abilities you've developed through use or practice.

Example: If people frequently tell you that you make them laugh, your purpose involves being an encouragement or helping others feel at ease. Not everyone has this talent.

I - Insights: *"What life lessons have you learned that could help others?"*

Example: I grew up in an environment where we were always aware of our surroundings. Dr. Eric Thomas discusses how growing up in a tough neighborhood enhances deductive reasoning skills. For instance, if we were hanging out and saw someone running past us, we wouldn't stop to ask, "What are you running from?" We'd start running, too. We had the insight to act quickly and ask questions later.

G - Gifts: *"What comes naturally to you, even if it seems small?"*

Gifts are natural tendencies or inclinations you may not have worked for—they just *flow.*

Example: If you excel in math and find it easy to solve problems, this could be one of your gifts. You may not need to study as hard in that subject, which could indicate that you're naturally gifted in that area. Different temperaments are better suited to various subjects, and knowing yours will help you identify your unique strengths.

E - Experiences: *"How have your challenges shaped your strengths?"*

Example: Growing up, my family didn't have a lot of money. The six of us lived in a two-bedroom apartment in the Projects for years. Not having the financial freedom I wanted taught me how to be resourceful and get the most out of free programs. This experience has been invaluable in business because I know how to get the greatest return on a small investment. It also gave me the confidence to know that even if something is outside my budget, I can find ways to earn money or leverage my skills to get what I need.

R - Resources: *"What do you have access to that could help you grow—and maybe even give you an edge?"*

You may not realize it, but you already have access to tools, spaces, or people that can support your goals. These are your resources—and when used wisely, they can help you walk in purpose with confidence.

Example: Think about where you live. Maybe you're in a rural area with open land, trails, and nature all around you. That's access to peace, clarity, and even movement—things that fuel your mind and body.

Or you could live in a city with public transportation, free workshops, museums, or local mentors who host events. Don't overlook these community gems—they could be the very stepping stones you need to get to your next level.

Sometimes, your biggest resource is your proximity to people who inspire you. You might live in the same city as someone you admire or attend the same school, church, or community center. Showing up to their events, volunteering, or just being in the room can open doors.

Your life matters, and living by your purpose will help make the world a better place. Dr. Dharius Daniels discusses how purpose is often connected to something in the world that bothers you, something you want to change or improve. For example, if seeing people hungry breaks your heart, perhaps your calling is to feed people experiencing homelessness. By answering that call, you can positively impact your community in ways you may not even predict.

Growing up, I had a guided notebook where I recorded milestones each year. At the start of each school year, I filled out prompts like "What is your height?" "What is your favorite subject?" and "What do you want to be when you grow up?" I remember looking back at this book in middle school and seeing a different answer each year. When I was younger, I wanted to be whatever I saw around me—dancers, doctors, lawyers—even if they didn't look like me.

Playing basketball in middle school sparked my interest in a career in the sport. After attending sessions with PowerPlay, I expanded my vision to include the possibility of working in sports beyond the court, perhaps in the corporate offices as an executive. I did not know that although about 11-15 people may play for an NBA or WNBA team, upwards of 250 people could work for that one team in several different departments. Further, thinking about the number of teams in both American professional leagues and brands even connected to the team doesn't scratch the surface of how many opportunities there are to work in basketball alone, off the court. Seeing women of color working at ESPN, Major League Baseball, and other prominent organizations in a variety of roles opened my eyes to options I had not considered.

I attended Hampton University and tried out for the Division 1 Lady Pirates basketball team. Despite my "skills," I didn't get a call back (they must have lost my phone number!). That moment made me rethink my "hoop dreams" and my hopes of playing in the WNBA. I also tried to get into the Scripps School of Journalism, but I didn't make the cut there either.

At this point, I had to choose another major. After praying and fasting for three days, I felt that God was guiding me to listen to my mom and my heart. When I spoke to my mom about changing my major, she suggested Sport Management, noting how PowerPlay had impacted me and how the field might offer a good income.

Initially, I hesitated because I saw Sport Management as a field for athletes. I didn't want to pursue something just for the money. But after praying, I felt at peace about making the change. I had already gained valuable insights from my experiences at PowerPlay, and my time as an athlete equipped me with skills in teamwork and leadership despite my high school team's limited playoff success.

When I went to the Head of the Sport Management Department, the entire process was the smoothest experience I had at school. I later learned that I could graduate with my bachelor's in three years instead of four. During this time, I began to understand what it meant to know my purpose. I realized I could make an impact in the field of sports, especially as a Black woman executive, because there were so few of us working off the court. I went on to receive the Sports Management Major of the Year award upon graduation. As a recipient of this award, the head of our department, Dr. Ralph Charlton, asked the Physical Education Major of the Year recipient and me to present with him at the North American Society for Sport Management (NASSM) conference in Chicago, Illinois. My mom even met me in Chicago, which was a treat.

Further, I spent over ten years as a sports journalist after college, covering events and writing for publications such as Black Enterprise, NBC News, SLAM magazine, ESPNW, Bleacher Report, and more.

Living a purpose-driven life will help you keep going when you feel like giving up. It will remind you that your life is bigger than yourself. The obstacles you've overcome are tied to your purpose. You survived them, and now you can share with others how they can do the same.

Purpose Isn't Found—It's Revealed Over Time

The more you walk it out, the more it makes sense.

Reflections

1. What problems in the world, big or small, do you feel called to help solve?

2. What does "purpose" mean to you right now—and how has that definition changed over time?

Using the TIGER method:

- T- What is one talent others often notice in you?

- I- What insight have you gained from your life that could help someone else?

- G- What gift comes naturally to you?

- E- What experience has prepared you for the purpose you're growing into?

- R- What resource or advantage do you have access to right now?

PART 4

WIN

10. Goal Setting: Turning Your Dreams into Reality

Imagine a woman walking up to a ticket counter at an airport. She asks for a ticket, but when the agent inquires about her destination, she has no answer. Where will she go? Nowhere if she doesn't have a destination.

Dreams don't work unless you do—and setting a goal is the first step.

When I heard the New Jersey Nets were moving to Brooklyn, my heart dropped. Whaaat?! As a Brooklyn native and lifelong basketball fan (still forever faithful to my NY Knicks), I immediately thought, *I have to be part of making this vision a reality.*

Having an NBA team come to my hometown wasn't just exciting—it felt personal. I saw it as an opportunity to connect my love of sports with my desire to serve my community. So, I set a goal. I wrote it down. In 2010, I declared that by the time Barclays Center opened in 2012, I would be involved in a meaningful way. I also acknowledged the displacement and changes happening in Brooklyn, and committed that if I were to be involved, I would use my role to give back and uplift.

At the time, I was working at The High School for Sports Management and passed the Barclays Center construction site daily on my way to the school. Each time, I'd say to myself, *There will be a role for me in that building.* I stayed in touch with a woman I'd met early on—she wasn't working with the Nets when we met, but shortly after we met, she joined their team. I kept reading articles about the move, stayed updated on all the developments, and even attended Nets games in New

Jersey, while living in Brooklyn, just to connect with staff and learn more. At one of those games, I met Brett Yormark, the CEO of the team at the time. I was planting seeds—networking, showing up, and staying ready.

Then it happened. A few months before the arena opened, I received an email from the same woman I'd stayed connected with over the years. She had been asked to find someone who could serve as a bridge between the arena and the Brooklyn community and she said, I was the first person that came to her mind.

Quick note: People always say, it's not WHAT you know, but WHO you know. I believe that it's not just about WHO you know, but who knows YOU. Staying in touch with people, especially not only reaching out to them when you need something, can be beneficial when pursuing your goals.

Soon after reconnecting with my contact, I was hired as the arena's first Community Manager. My team and I all were at the Jay Z concert on opening night. In that role, I had the chance to create real impact, not only in professional basketball, but in college basketball, music, hockey, and boxing. We launched initiatives that reached thousands of students and organizations. I created and hosted an annual Back-to-School Bash, inviting some of the same nonprofits that once poured into me and I brought two Brooklyn Nets players to my former high school to inspire the next generation.

Over the three and a half years I was with the organization, my dream came to life—and so did the dreams of others I was able to support along the way.

Setting goals is like choosing your destination—it gives you a sense of direction. Purpose answers the WHY of your journey, but goals help you figure out the HOW to reach where you want to be. Without goals, you'll wander.

One of the best ways to achieve your goals is through Study, Practice, and Observation (SPO), a concept I first learned from Dr. A.R. Bernard, Sr.

Study:

- Research the area or topic you want to focus on. To achieve a goal, you need to understand the path that will get you there.
- Example: When I decided to attend graduate school, I didn't just apply to any program. I researched various universities, reached out to mentors, and even traveled to Cambridge for a Harvard recruitment event for students of color. Studying helped me prepare for what was to come.

Practice:

- Goals require consistent effort. Consistency builds momentum. Even small, daily actions can lead to significant results over time.
- Example: As a dancer, I dreamed of mastering the movements like the Pas De Bourrée. I committed to stretching every day. It didn't happen immediately, but over time, I achieved an outstanding posture and flawless execution.

Observation:

- Learn from those who have achieved similar goals. When I aspired to become a video jockey (VJ), I had no mentor in that field, and I didn't have YouTube or podcasts focused on it as there are today. This experience taught me the importance of surrounding myself with people who could guide me.

- Example: At the Harvard recruitment event, I observed how students and faculty interacted and presented themselves. This gave me valuable insights into positioning myself for success.

Setting SMART Goals

Once you've taken time to study your goals, practice regularly, and observe others who've walked the path before you, it's time to set a plan in motion. One of the most effective ways to do this is by using the SMART goal framework—a method I first learned in high school that I've carried with me ever since.

- Specific: Clearly defined. Know exactly what you want to accomplish.
  Example: Instead of saying, "*I want to go to college*," say, "*I want to attend Hampton University.*"
- Measurable: Ensure you can track your progress.
  Example: "I will complete three college applications by December 1st."
- Achievable: Set goals that challenge you but are realistic based on time and resources.
  Example: If you're currently mainly earning Cs, aiming for all As next semester might require extra study hours or tutoring. Balancing other responsibilities, such as sports or work, means you may need to adjust your expectations or plan to ensure you're not overwhelmed.
- Relevant: Align your goals with your bigger purpose.
  Example: If your purpose is to help others, setting a

goal to join the student government or volunteer at a local food bank aligns with that vision.

- Time-bound: Set a deadline and stay focused.
  Example: *I will improve my math grade by the end of this semester.*

SMART goals help break down big dreams into manageable steps.

Goals in Action

- Dancing: When I was at the East New York Theatrical Workshop, I set a goal to learn the splits. Every day, I practiced stretching. It was the discipline and consistency that helped me achieve this goal.
- College: In high school, I set SMART goals to get into college. I studied for standardized tests, wrote application essays, applied for scholarships, and spoke to current college students and graduates to learn from their experiences.
- Graduate School: Attending Harvard wasn't just a dream—it was a goal I worked toward. I sought mentors, attended recruitment events, and acted on the advice I received. Meeting the head of my department wasn't a coincidence; it was a direct result of intentional effort.

Not every goal will come to fruition (like my dream of becoming a VJ on MTV), but every goal teaches you something valuable in the process.

Having a mentor can be the difference between success and failure. When I set my sights on graduate school, I reached out to people who had been through the process before me. They offered advice, shared resources, and helped me network. Goals are much easier to achieve when someone is guiding you.

Healthy Goal-Setting Habits

- Write your goals down and display them where you will see them daily.
  Example: Place a sticky note that says "I will graduate with a 3.5 GPA" on your desk or by your bed. Look at it and read it aloud every day.
- Break your goals into smaller tasks.
  Example: If your goal is to graduate with a 3.5 GPA, smaller tasks include reaching out to a tutor, asking successful students how they study, watching YouTube videos on study strategies, or ensuring you're studying in a distraction-free environment.
- Celebrate your progress, even the small wins.
  Example: When you get a good grade on a test, treat yourself to something you love—a favorite meal, a small item from a store, or just a walk in your favorite park. Rewarding yourself reinforces positive behavior.

Living with purpose means living intentionally. One of the best ways to live intentionally is by having goals and plans that align with your dreams. I have wanted to make an impact and to help those organizations and people that helped me on my journey and I was able to do that in my role at Barclays Center.

Goals are the actions that bring your purpose to life. Study, practice, and observe. Set SMART goals. Write them down.

Take consistent steps every day. Remember, the journey may not always be easy, but each step you take brings you closer to realizing your dreams.

Dreams Stay Dreams Until You Turn Them Into Goals

Now it's your turn to map out the HOW.

Challenge for the Reader

Right now, think of one goal that aligns with your purpose. Write it down and make it SMART:

- What is one of your goals?
- How will you measure success?
- Which action steps will you take daily or weekly to help you achieve your goal?
- What's your deadline?

11. Culture Consciousness

When I worked at the New York Knicks offices at Madison Square Garden, I started each day with what I thought was a simple, friendly gesture: saying "good morning" to my colleagues. But to my surprise, I was asked to stop saying hi to at least one person in particular. It wasn't personal—it just wasn't the culture of that environment. People weren't always in the mood for early-morning greetings. While my energy wasn't wrong, it clashed with the unspoken standards around me.

This experience taught me an important lesson: understanding how to read the room and having enough awareness of the culture within it are crucial in deciding whether or not to adapt to the social norms of your environment. This is a key element in social mobility. Whether it's at work, in school, or among peers, being attuned to the culture of the space you occupy can have a significant impact on how you're perceived and how effective you are as a team player.

Social Etiquette: Adapting Without Losing Yourself

1. Be Aware of Your Surroundings

Adapting doesn't mean changing who you are by any means— conformity is NOT the goal—it's about observing the unspoken rules of the space you're in. For example, when entering a new school, workplace, or social group, take time to observe:

- How do people interact?
- What are their routines and rhythms?
- What's considered appropriate versus disruptive?

It's not about changing who you are but how you show up to fit the situation.

2. Dress the Part

First impressions matter. In new environments, how you dress communicates a message. When I transitioned from high school to entering professional and academic spaces, I had to learn what was appropriate for each setting while still embracing my own personal style. Dressing appropriately shows respect for the local culture and environment. It can give you the confidence to focus on achieving your goals.

3. Study the Culture

At one point, I attended a school with a culture so rigorous that earning a "C" was practically seen as a failure. I didn't know how to study effectively when I first started, and I had to learn quickly. Similarly, in the professional world, understanding the "rules of success"—whether it's meeting deadlines, arriving early, or networking—can make a significant difference in how you're perceived and how you succeed.

Social Cues and Office Etiquette

Every environment has its own unique language, and understanding it is essential for navigating new spaces effectively. Here are some practical tips:

- Social Cues: Pay attention to body language and tone of voice. If someone seems focused or stressed, it might not be the best time to share a joke or ask a question.

- Office Etiquette: Small details, like the wording of emails or how meetings are conducted, provide clues about what's expected of you.

- Know How You're Perceived: Perception often becomes a reality in many environments. Take feedback seriously, and if you're unsure how you're coming across, don't hesitate to ask for constructive input.

From the Hood to Harvard: Bridging Two Worlds

When I transitioned from the hood to Harvard, I faced a steep learning curve. I didn't know how to study, and the academic rigor was overwhelming to me at first. But with time, I figured out how to adapt while staying true to myself. My goals were clear: I wanted to thrive, not just survive. That meant learning the unwritten rules of the culture I was now a part of. Note that I would also expect the same of someone who was coming from Harvard and going to 'the hood.' The culture should be studied and respected, not gentrified. It works both ways.

Whether your goal is academic success, career advancement, or personal growth, adaptability is crucial. But adapting does not mean erasing who you are. It's about finding harmony between your personality and the expectations of the environment around you.

Understanding Social Etiquette as a Tool for Success

To achieve your goals, you need to understand and respect the culture, norms, and routines of the environments you enter. Being adaptable doesn't mean shrinking yourself; it means being strategic about how you show up. Success comes when you align your actions with the standards around you while staying true to your core values.

Reflecting on my time at the Knicks, I now understand that respecting other people's personalities and routines is just as important as sharing my own. I learned that sometimes holding back my energy was the best way to be a better teammate. Adapting to the culture around me wasn't about silencing myself or being inauthentic—it was about finding the best way to contribute and achieve my goals.

It's Not About Shrinking—It's About Showing Up Strategically

Now let's reflect on how you can thrive without losing yourself.

1. Have you ever entered a space (school, job, or group) where the culture felt unfamiliar or unspoken? How did you adjust—or not—and what did you learn from that experience?

2. What's one environment you're currently in where you could observe more before acting? What might you look for?

3. How do you define the difference between *adapting* and *conforming*?

4. What is one piece of feedback you've received— positive or constructive—that helped you better navigate an environment?

5. How do you honor your authentic self while also respecting the expectations of a new space?

12. Winning: Being Ready for Change

Change is the only constant in life.

N ow that you've learned how to discover your personality type, set goals, and understand different cultures and environments, it's important to remember that your plans will evolve. The road to success is always under construction, and you never know what might come along the route.

Life is less about what happens to us and more about how we respond to what happens. Every cause has an effect, and sometimes, that cause comes from other people, nature, society, government, or even ourselves. While we may not always control what happens to us, we can almost always control our response to it. How we respond to challenges will determine how we move forward. If we understand that setbacks are often setups for comebacks and we take the time to assess situations before reacting, we can and will thrive.

I recall breaking my foot just a month into my sophomore year of high school. I didn't injure it playing basketball but instead by falling into a ditch at a youth retreat. I was on crutches for about six weeks, and I didn't expect my high school career to begin without the full use of both of my legs (sigh). I had to get braids because I kept sweating my relaxed hair out when going up and down five flights of stairs at my high school when the elevator didn't work. But there I was. I couldn't stay home. My goals were too big to make a small setback keep me down and make me fall behind.

I could have let this setback frustrate me for the entire time I was in the cast. Although I was initially upset, I realized that I still possessed many abilities. Instead of dwelling on bitterness, I chose to focus on gratitude. This mindset helped me excel in the classroom and meet new friends. Once my foot healed, I even joined the girls' basketball team.

Contentment Vs. Satisfaction

One of my mentees, Janay, once asked me how I felt about being content but still wanting more. I used to work for a CEO who often said, "I'm happy but not satisfied." His words stuck with me and came to mind when I thought about the answer to this question.

Contentment and a desire for more are not mutually exclusive. You can practice gratitude while still setting goals and striving for bigger dreams. In fact, gratitude is one of the best ways to attract more of what you want in life. Those who are faithful with few can be trusted with many. On the journey to achieving our dreams, we must also take stock of where we are and how far we've come before looking ahead to the future.

As Bill Keane said, "Yesterday is history, tomorrow is a mystery, today is a gift of God, which is why we call it the present."

Life can be unpredictable. You can plan every step, set every goal, and work hard—but curveballs will come. The key is learning how to navigate life with grace and gratitude, finding contentment in the present while staying driven to achieve your goals.

Caution Against Comparison

Comparison is the thief of joy.

This saying serves as a reminder to avoid comparing ourselves to others, especially when it comes to social media. People often share only their highlights online—what they've achieved, what they're doing, and how their lives appear perfect. What they don't show is the journey or struggle it took to get there.

One thing that can make us feel discontent is comparison. When we compare our journeys to others, we risk:

1. Losing focus on our own goals.
2. Giving an unfair assessment of our own success by only measuring it against what someone else chooses to share.

Be mindful of how you interact with others' social media presence. Oftentimes, it doesn't reflect their whole story.

Contentment vs. Satisfaction: What's the Difference?

- Contentment is finding peace in the present. It's about appreciating where you are, even if it's not perfect. It's about being grateful for what you have.
- Satisfaction is the feeling you get when you achieve your goals. It's what motivates you to keep striving for more.

You need both to live fully. If you only chase satisfaction, you'll always feel like something's missing. If you focus solely on contentment, you may stop striving for growth. Balance is key. Be content with your journey, but remain hungry for growth.

Loss

Life is precious, and we only get one of them. I encourage you to live it fully while you can. Unfortunately, I learned firsthand how quickly life plans can change when I lost my partner and friend, Luc. Gabby shared that he had planned to propose to me about a month after the time of his passing. He had all the qualities I wanted in a man and was someone I thought I'd spend the rest of my life with. But he passed away suddenly while on vacation with his friends.

Drake once said, "Everybody dies, but not everybody lives," and Luc truly lived—he embraced every moment. After his passing, things I used to stress over felt trivial in the bigger picture. I began asking myself, *"Does this really matter?"* When life throws you curveballs, practicing gratitude for what you still have doesn't erase the pain, but it gives you perspective.

Resilience: Remaining Hopeful Despite Setbacks

Tragedy and setbacks are part of life, but they don't define you.

- When my partner passed away, I had to rebuild my sense of hope.

- When I lost my job due to restructuring, I felt a sense of defeat. But that loss forced me to adapt and find new opportunities I hadn't considered before. That's how I landed a role at NBC News' NBC BLK.

You won't always have control over what happens, but you can control how you respond to it. Staying hopeful—even when things don't go as planned—will help you move forward.

Life is About the Big Picture

When I failed the test to get into journalism school in college, it felt like the end of the world. At that moment, I couldn't see how that failure was shaping me into a stronger person. Looking back, I see it as a launchpad. That failure didn't stop me from writing, creating, or pursuing my dreams—it made me more determined. Eventually, I worked as a journalist for top publications and was flown across the country to cover events such as NBA All-Star Weekend for eight years, the Black Enterprise Golf & Tennis Challenge, and special events for Nike, Reebok, and Under Armour.

Life is full of moments that feel like failures, but they're often detours on the path to success. They're opportunities to shift, adapt, and grow.

Living Fully

Living fully means embracing both the highs and the lows, as well as the successes and the failures. It means setting goals and pursuing them with passion while also finding joy in the little moments along the way.

Gratitude, hope, and resilience are your tools for navigating life's unpredictability. Use them to strike a balance between contentment and satisfaction. Life won't always go as planned, but every twist and turn brings a lesson worth learning.

You Can't Predict the Storm—But You Can Choose to Glow Anyway

Take a moment to reflect on your journey, your growth, and what really matters most.

Reflections: What Really Matters

If you remember nothing else, remember this: life is about growth, gratitude, and living with purpose. Be content with where you are, stay hopeful for where you're going, and always take the time to appreciate the journey.

1. As you close this book, think about your own life. What are you striving for? What drives you?

2. What lessons will you carry forward as you pursue your own dreams?

3. What are you grateful for?

4. Think of a time when something unexpected happened in your life. What did you learn from it?

5. What's one way you can remind yourself to *glow anyway* when life doesn't go as planned?

You Glow Girl

You've walked through stories.
You've reflected on who you are.
You've seen how your dreams, your voice, and your choices
matter.

Now carry the glow forward.

Glow with wisdom.
Glow with joy.
Glow with boldness.
Glow with grace.

Glow for the ones watching you.
Glow for the dreams still growing in you.
Glow because the world needs your light.

You're not just becoming a shining star.
You are one.

And that changes everything.

Resources

Temperament Overview

To learn more about the basic types of temperament and how they influence personality, see articles on psychology reference sites such as Britannica.com.

Sensory Support Ideas

Some of the self-care visuals and calming tools were inspired by resources like the Sensory TheraPlay Box blog, which provides ideas for sensory-friendly play and daily routines.

Historical Perspective on Temperament

The ancient Greek physician Galen proposed a four-temperament model based on bodily fluids, an early attempt to explain personality traits. While outdated today, it's still referenced in temperament discussions as a starting point in personality theory.

Music Mentioned

The song "Little Girl" by Mary Mary is referenced in this book. For lyrics and emotional inspiration, you can find the official version on major streaming platforms.

Acknowledgments

First and foremost, I thank God, without whom I could do nothing. My parents—Mom and Dad—for your unwavering love, prayers, and sacrifices. I truly would not be here without you. To my late grandmother, Leona Hall, thank you for planting in me a deep love for books, family, and storytelling. Your spirit continues to guide me. To my sister Jhanee and my nephew Massari—you inspire me every day. I'm grateful for my Aunt Elvera and her son, my cousin Michael, who lived with me for much of my childhood and has been like a brother to me.

I am also thankful for my Aunt Cherise and Uncle Darren and my cousins Maleek, Nicole, Darren Jr. (Lil D), Kyana, Kataleya, Butch, Teddy, GiGi, Gina, Tashona and my Smart family. Thank you Larone. I'm blessed by my Gary family: Angie B., Adrianne, Antoine, Darnell, Kevin, Eric, Terica, the late Tonda—and the "Dips, Chips, and Tips." To the New Breed—my dad's crew of godchildren—Tiffany, Charisma, Rhonda, Kera, Kara, Indya, Quianna, and Monique—love ya'll. To Pink Houses, DC37, PS 273, and Russell Sage.

To my friends who have left an impact on this book and my life: Gabby, thank you for writing the foreword. Aleea, my very first co-author, and the rest of the original 'Fab Five of HU,' Chivon, Atiya and ebi. Carla - thank you for your literary advice.

The group of Harry Van Arsdale, Jr. High School: China, Omar, Sam, Shaulette, Tamika, plus Ashley and Tiffany— thank you for your love and support. To the Dobson family, thank you for treating me as one of your own. To the rest of my *50 Summers* family—Andrew, Donnie, Ed, Kareen, and

Michelle—plus the Cudjoes and the Wilkes—thank you for being in my corner.

To my pastors Dr. A.R. Bernard and Pastor Jamaal Bernard, thank you for the many years of wisdom and principles you've poured into me and the CCC and C3 family—Gloria, Lisa, Minister Dario, Minister Reggie, Minister Chris, Minister Malissa, Minister Aaron, Brother Keith, Aisha Joshida—you all helped shape my spiritual and personal growth, and for that, I'm forever grateful. To Faithful Central Bible Church—thank you for letting me launch my first Brown Girls Glow Programming, and to my Double Love Experience and Change Church families, where I am happy to continue to serve. Further, to the women of my prayer groups in Brooklyn, Harvard, Los Angeles, and Atlanta, you have been a light and treasure.

To my mentors, Dr. Ellen M., Alfred Edmond, Jr., Beth R., Karin B., April W., Rolanda G., Joi G., Juliette G., thank you for pouring into me. To my thoughtful mentors, LaChina Robinson, Dr. Ni'cola Mitchell, and Deniese Davis—I appreciate you all and thank you for your quotes, kind words and insights.

To my high school teachers and guides who shaped me at a pivotal time in my life, Ms. Valentine, the late Mr. Peters and his daughter and my mentor Ashley, Ms. Gentile, Mr. Raubvogel, Mr. Martin, Ms. Huguet, and Ms. Janvier—thank you for seeing something in me. To my Hampton University friends and professors, Dr. Charlton, and to former President Dr. Harvey—thank you for believing in the power of student potential. To my Harvard professors and mentors, Dr. Schwager, Dr. Lawrence Lightfoot, and Kristen.

To Eric Thomas, Ph.D., and CJ—you encouraged me to speak to the young women who are just like I once was and continually inspire me. Thank you. To my ETA and Game Changers crew—Candis, Karl, Nicky, Jemal, Ms. DeDe, the Lemon Squeeze—thank you for cheering me on early in my speaking journey and beyond. To Marshawn Evans Daniels— thank you for modeling how to build a business *God's way*. I'm grateful for your example.

To the incredible supervisors who gave me opportunities and taught me so much: Donna Orender, Dr. Robin Pitts, Dr. Allison Farrington, Reverend Branch, Petra Pope, Elisa Padilla, Anslem Samuel Rocque, Amber Payne, Steve Harvey, Melinda, Sofia, Shaniece, Ianthe, Shane, Shay and Christel— thank you.

To my Parables From The Projects Productions mentors, Sonya White, Matty Rich, and Booker T. Mattison, and to my school, NYU and New York Film Academy—I would not be where I am on my film journey without you. To my clients and collaborators, including J Smiles and my teammates—thank you for trusting me with your stories.

To my coach Shana, Shantel, and everyone else who has supported me throughout the years and helped me to bring this book to life—whether through prayer, encouragement, feedback, or support—I see you. I thank you. I love you.

Author Bio

Mia Hall is a passionate storyteller and advocate for young women, dedicated to empowering teenage girls to be more confident, courageous, and convinced that they can achieve their biggest dreams. With nearly two decades of experience mentoring young women of color from marginalized communities, Mia draws from her extensive career as a journalist and producer for leading outlets such as NBC News, Black Enterprise, ESPN, SLAM Magazine, and Bleacher Report to inspire and uplift others.

Her debut book, *Glow Girl: Empowering Teenage Girls to Grow, Lead, Overcome, and Win*, is the culmination of Mia's commitment to addressing the real-life challenges teenage girls often face—especially those from underrepresented communities.

When she's not producing films, writing, or mentoring, Mia enjoys traveling, hiking, and serving in ministry. A former basketball player, she still loves hitting the court for a great workout.

To learn more about Mia and her mission, visit miahalltv.com. For inspiration and updates on her work in media and with young women around the world, subscribe to her YouTube channel: @miahalltv.

GLOW GIRL

Let Glow Girl help unlock confidence, purpose, and a world of new possibilities for every young woman ready to glow.

Glow Girl: Empowering Teenage Girls to Grow, Lead, Overcome, and Win is more than just a book; it's a transformative toolkit to self-discovery, leadership, and confidence, inspiring every young woman to shine brightly.

Glow Girl goes beyond advice—it equips readers to take action, face their fears, and embrace their unique power. Mia's authentic voice and uplifting narratives bring a powerful blend of relatable stories and actionable strategies, creating a guide that feels like a mentor, coach, and big sister all in one.

Whether you're a teen dreaming of a brighter future, a parent encouraging your daughter, or an educator seeking to uplift the next generation, Glow Girl is the ultimate companion.

Praise for Mia Hall and Glow Girl

"Bottom line: You need to buy copies of Mia Hall's book, Glow Girl!: A Guide for Teenage Girls to Grow, Learn, Overcome, and Win, for every pre-teen and teen girl in your family, community, and personal network of influence. As a bona fide girl dad with a lifetime commitment to mentorship, I would have given this book to my now-adult daughters and nieces when they were teens. Since Mia's time as a college undergrad, when she first claimed me as a mentor, she has been Exhibit A of the indisputable fact that #mymenteesarebetterthanyours. There is none better suited than Mia to serve as a role model and source of sound advice for

teen girls, and no better resource than Glow Girl! to ensure that they will benefit from her example."

–Alfred Edmond Jr., #TheSuccesspert, SVP/Executive Editor, BLACK ENTERPRISE, Host, Mocha Podcasts Network

"Since I first met Mia, there has been one consistent theme to her life's work: to empower young girls and women. This book will carry the inspirational message of community, perseverance, and intentional growth that Mia has lived in her own life, and now passes on to the young women coming behind her."

–LaChina Robinson, ESPN Analyst, Co-Founder, Rising Media Stars

"GLOW GIRL is the ultimate guide for every young woman with big dreams. Mia candidly shares her journey that will leave you inspired and confident! I wish it existed when I was a teen, so it's a real treat for today's generation."

–Deniese Davis, CEO/Founder, Reform Media Group

"A girl's power isn't given—it's already within her, waiting to shine. When she believes in herself, no obstacle is too great, and no dream is too far. She grows through challenges, learns from experience, overcomes with strength, and wins by simply never giving up.
Get Glow, Girl! because your light was meant to shine!"

– Dr. Ni'Cola Mitchell, Bestselling Author, Founder - Girls Who Brunch Tour

Join this inspiring journey of growth and leadership.

Notes

Notes

Notes

Notes

Notes

Notes

Notes

Notes

Notes

Notes

Notes

www.ingramcontent.com/pod-product-compliance
Lightning Source LLC
Chambersburg PA
CBHW051540120626
46551CB00013B/1303

* 9 7 9 8 9 9 9 4 8 3 8 0 5 *